Date: 4/14/21

J BIO LIZZO
London, Martha,
Lizzo /

WWW.FOCUSREADERS.COM

Copyright © 2021 by Focus Readers®, Lake Elmo, MN 55042. All rights reserved. No part of this book may be reproduced or utilized in any form or by any means without written permission from the publisher.

Focus Readers is distributed by North Star Editions:
sales@northstareditions.com | 888-417-0195

Produced for Focus Readers by Red Line Editorial.

Photographs ©: Brent N. Clarke/Invision/AP Images, cover, 1; Matt Sayles/Invision/AP Images, 4–5, 7, 27; Shutterstock Images, 8–9, 20–21, 29; zz/KGC-138/STAR MAX/IPx/AP Images, 10, 12; Rob Latour/Invision/AP Images, 14–15; Amy Harris/Invision/AP Images, 17; Richard Shotwell/Invision/AP Images, 18; Owen Sweeney/Invision/AP Images, 23; Chris Pizzello/Invision/AP Images, 25

Library of Congress Cataloging-in-Publication Data
Names: London, Martha, author.
Title: Lizzo / by Martha London.
Description: Lake Elmo, MN : Focus Readers, 2021. | Series: Biggest names in music | Includes index. | Audience: Grades 4-6
Identifiers: LCCN 2020005928 (print) | LCCN 2020005929 (ebook) | ISBN 9781644936351 (hardcover) | ISBN 9781644936443 (paperback) | ISBN 9781644936627 (pdf) | ISBN 9781644936535 (ebook)
Subjects: LCSH: Lizzo, 1988---Juvenile literature. | Singers--United States--Biography--Juvenile literature. | Rap musicians--United States--Biography--Juvenile literature.
Classification: LCC ML3930.L579 L66 2021 (print) | LCC ML3930.L579 (ebook) | DDC 782.421649092 [B]--dc23
LC record available at https://lccn.loc.gov/2020005928
LC ebook record available at https://lccn.loc.gov/2020005929

Printed in the United States of America
Mankato, MN
082020

ABOUT THE AUTHOR
Martha London writes books for young readers full-time. She enjoys all types of music. In high school and college, she spent several years performing in musicals.

TABLE OF CONTENTS

CHAPTER 1
The VMAs 5

CHAPTER 2
Midwest to Texas 9

CHAPTER 3
A New Way to Play 15

CHAPTER 4
Pushing Boundaries 21

Lizzo At-a-Glance • 28
Focus on Lizzo • 30
Glossary • 31
To Learn More • 32
Index • 32

CHAPTER 1

THE VMAS

The lights came up. People in the audience cheered. Lizzo stood onstage at the 2019 MTV Video Music Awards (VMAs). She was **nominated** for several awards. They included Best New Artist, Song of the Summer, and Power **Anthem**.

Music began to play. Lizzo started singing her hit song "Truth Hurts."

Lizzo sings at the MTV VMAs in August 2019.

After the song ended, the music changed. Behind Lizzo, women with Afros streamed onstage. They formed a V behind her. Lizzo started singing her feel-good anthem "Good as Hell." The crowd sang along. People jumped up and down in time with the beat.

Near the end of the song, Lizzo took a break from singing. She spoke to the audience. She said she knew not everyone always feels good about themselves. But she reminded people that loving themselves was important. Lizzo invited the audience to sing with her. She asked how everyone was feeling. She held out the microphone to hear the crowd's

Lizzo performs with backup dancers at the VMAs.

answer. Then she joined her dancers and finished the song.

The crowd cheered for Lizzo's performance. Lizzo had been performing for six years. But people were finally starting to notice her. Lizzo was a hit.

CHAPTER 2

MIDWEST TO TEXAS

Lizzo's real name is Melissa Jefferson. She was born on April 27, 1988, in Detroit, Michigan. Melissa spent half of her childhood in Detroit. **Gospel music** was an early inspiration for her. She sang in a church choir. Melissa loved music. But for most of elementary school, she didn't see herself as a musician.

Lizzo performed at Rule Breakers 2019, a festival celebrating musicians and trailblazers.

Lizzo dances during a performance in London, England, in 2019.

She wanted to be a scientist or a writer. Melissa didn't take music seriously until she was older.

When Melissa was nine years old, she moved to Houston, Texas, with her parents and older siblings. Melissa discovered many new types of music in Houston. She also found that she was good at freestyle rap. She could think up rhymes quickly. And she could rap them on the spot.

A DATE WITH DESTINY

When Melissa was in fifth grade, she went to a Destiny's Child concert. Destiny's Child was an all-women R&B group. *R&B* stands for rhythm and blues. It's a type of music that combines many other forms, including gospel and blues. After that concert, Melissa knew she wanted to make music. When her school's band director asked if she wanted to learn how to play the flute, Melissa said yes. She joined the band program.

Lizzo still plays her flute, which she calls Sasha. The flute even has its own Instagram account.

In high school, Melissa got the nickname "Lisso" when her friends shortened her name. She formed her first all-girl rap group. It was called Cornrow Clique. The Jay-Z song "Izzo" was popular when Cornrow Clique was making music.

Eventually, the name "Lisso" became "Lizzo."

Lizzo joined the marching band in high school. She described herself as a nerd. Playing in band wasn't considered cool by some students. But Lizzo loved playing the flute. She wanted to keep improving. Lizzo wanted to keep playing no matter what other kids thought.

Lizzo's practice paid off. She received a music scholarship for college. That means the college paid for her to attend it. But Lizzo didn't like college. She decided that she wanted to perform her own music. Lizzo chose to quit college in order to focus on her music.

CHAPTER 3

A NEW WAY TO PLAY

Lizzo didn't have a lot of money after quitting college. In fact, she didn't have a home for several months. She slept on her friends' couches. Then, in 2010, her father died. Lizzo struggled with **depression**. She moved to Denver, Colorado, to live with her mother.

Lizzo has overcome many challenges to become the superstar that she is today.

In 2011, Lizzo was ready to move again. One of Lizzo's friends suggested she move to Minneapolis, Minnesota. The friend talked about the music scene there. She thought Lizzo would be happy in Minnesota. There were opportunities for Lizzo to start performing again.

SELF-LOVE

In 2010, Lizzo was overexercising. She had an **eating disorder.** She called that time period the worst of her life. Lizzo worked hard to have a healthy body and mind. In 2019, she said she still struggles with self-love. Some people say her weight means she is not beautiful or healthy. But Lizzo knows that isn't true. Self-love is important to her. She wants to be a role model for others.

Lizzo and Sophia Eris perform at the Bonnaroo Music and Arts Festival in Tennessee in 2016.

Soon after moving to Minneapolis, Lizzo formed a rap group. GRRRL PRTY included Lizzo and another musician, Sophia Eris. They toured and performed together. It wasn't easy. GRRRL PRTY was a two-woman show. They drove the van and set up their equipment themselves.

Lizzo performs at the 2017 Billboard Music Awards in Los Angeles, California.

GRRRL PRTY gave Lizzo a chance to perform at many locations. She caught the attention of a **producer**. He offered Lizzo a contract with an indie **label**. *Indie* is short for independent. Independent labels are smaller than major labels.

Lizzo finished her first studio album with the label in 2013. *Lizzobangers* did not sell many copies. But it helped her increase her popularity. Lizzo finished another studio album in 2015 and an EP in 2016. An EP is a short album. It has fewer songs than a full-length album.

Lizzo's 2015 album had more success than *Lizzobangers*. *Big GRRRL Small World* got the attention of Atlantic Records. Atlantic Records is a major record label. It has a lot of money. It can support artists on a large scale. Atlantic Records offered Lizzo a contract. She accepted it. Lizzo moved to Los Angeles, California, to continue her career.

CHAPTER 4

PUSHING BOUNDARIES

In 2019, Lizzo released her first album with Atlantic Records. Many people thought the songs on *Cuz I Love You* were catchy. They thought the songs' messages were **empowering**. Three songs from the album became radio singles. That means they were released specifically for radio stations to play.

Lizzo owns the stage during her 2019 world tour.

Atlantic Records re-recorded the three singles for the radio. Lizzo's hard work had paid off.

Cuz I Love You has many songs that are personal for Lizzo. The songs talk about body image and self-acceptance. Lizzo has never been skinny. She is proud of her curves. She dresses in clothes that show

THE POWER OF MISSY

Missy Elliott is a black female rapper. Lizzo listened to Missy Elliott growing up. She saw that Elliott did not have to be skinny or white to be successful. Elliott's example helped Lizzo stay true to her body shape. Lizzo and Missy Elliott perform together on one of the songs in *Cuz I Love You*.

Lizzo doesn't think it is brave to love her body. But she is glad people see her as a role model.

off her body. Lizzo works to encourage acceptance of black bodies of all sizes.

Cuz I Love You received praise from **critics**. In addition, Lizzo received many honors and awards in 2019.

Time magazine named her Entertainer of the Year. She was nominated for three American Music Awards (AMAs). One of the nominations was for New Artist of the Year. Lizzo also was nominated for Best New Artist at the VMAs. And she received eight Grammy Award nominations. Lizzo had more Grammy nominations than any other artist that year. She won Best Pop Solo Performance for her song "Truth Hurts." She also won Best Traditional R&B Performance for her song "Jerome." And she won Best Urban Contemporary Album for *Cuz I Love You (Deluxe)*.

Lizzo also was nominated for six awards at the 2020 NAACP Image Awards.

Lizzo holds up her three awards at the 62nd Grammys.

This awards show is for musicians and actors of color. Lizzo won the award for Entertainer of the Year. She also received the Outstanding Music Video/Visual Album award for her song "Juice."

Lizzo's success has given her many opportunities. She uses her fame to help people. For example, in 2019, wildfires spread through Australia. Millions of acres burned. People and animals lost their homes. Lizzo performed at the FOMO Festival in Australia during her world tour. She raised money for local groups to help those hurt by the fires.

While in Australia, Lizzo also took a break from performing. She volunteered at a food bank. She packed boxes to donate to people who had lost their homes. Lizzo encouraged her fans to donate money. She also asked fans to raise awareness about the wildfires.

During her Grammy acceptance speech, Lizzo encouraged people to lift one another up during hard times.

Lizzo's music takes her all over the world. She works hard to empower people. Lizzo wants her music to make people feel good. But she also wants to make a difference. To her fans, she is already doing that.

AT-A-GLANCE

LIZZO

- Birth date: April 27, 1988
- Birthplace: Detroit, Michigan
- Family members: Shari (mother), Michael (father, deceased), Mikey (brother), Vanessa (sister)
- High school: Elsik High School
- Major accomplishments:
  - March 2016: Lizzo signs a contract with Atlantic Records.
  - September 2019: Lizzo's single "Truth Hurts" is No. 1 on *Billboard*'s Hot 100.
  - October 2019: Lizzo receives three AMAs nominations.
  - November 2019: Lizzo receives eight Grammy Award nominations.
  - January 2020: Lizzo receives six NAACP Image Awards nominations.

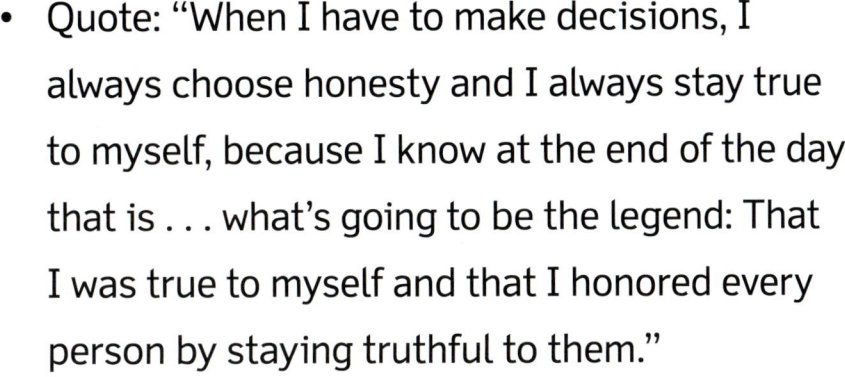

Lizzo takes the stage in Amsterdam, the Netherlands, in November 2019.

- Quote: "When I have to make decisions, I always choose honesty and I always stay true to myself, because I know at the end of the day that is . . . what's going to be the legend: That I was true to myself and that I honored every person by staying truthful to them."

Brittany Spanos. "How Lizzo Conquered Her Fears and Found Her Best Self." *Rolling Stone*. Penske Business Media, 19 Apr. 2019. Web. 17 Feb. 2020.

FOCUS ON
LIZZO

Write your answers on a separate piece of paper.

1. Write a paragraph summarizing the main ideas of Chapter 2.

2. Do you think it is important for musicians to talk about themes such as self-acceptance? Why or why not?

3. How many Grammy Award nominations did Lizzo receive in 2019?
    - **A.** two
    - **B.** six
    - **C.** eight

4. What might have happened if Lizzo had stayed with her indie label instead of working with Atlantic Records?
    - **A.** Fewer people would have heard her music.
    - **B.** She would have been nominated for more awards.
    - **C.** Her music would have gotten worse over time.

Answer key on page 32.

GLOSSARY

anthem
An inspiring popular song that is connected with a specific group, idea, or point of view.

critics
People who review music and give their thoughts on it.

depression
A medical condition of deep, long-lasting sadness or loss of interest.

eating disorder
A medical condition involving unhealthy eating patterns, such as eating too much or not enough.

empowering
Encouraging people to feel like they can do something.

gospel music
A type of religious music influenced by blues and folk songs.

label
A company that helps artists put out music.

nominated
Chosen as a finalist for an award or honor.

producer
A person who works with musicians to record songs.

TO LEARN MORE

BOOKS

Baxter, Roberta. *Women in Music*. Minneapolis: Abdo Publishing, 2019.

Klepeis, Alicia. *Music Trivia: What You Never Knew About Rock Stars, Recording Studios, and Smash-Hit Songs*. North Mankato, MN: Capstone Press, 2019.

Wilson, Lakita. *Lizzo: Breakout Artist*. Minneapolis: Lerner Publications, 2020.

NOTE TO EDUCATORS

Visit **www.focusreaders.com** to find lesson plans, activities, links, and other resources related to this title.

INDEX

American Music Awards (AMAs), 24
Atlantic Records, 19, 21–24

band, 11, 13
Big GRRRL Small World, 19

Cornrow Clique, 12
Cuz I Love You, 21–24

depression, 15
Destiny's Child, 11

eating disorder, 16
Elliott, Missy, 22
Eris, Sophia, 17

flute, 11, 13
FOMO Festival, 26
freestyle rap, 11

"Good as Hell," 6
gospel music, 9, 11
Grammy Awards, 24
GRRRL PRTY, 17–18

"Jerome," 24
"Juice," 25

Lizzobangers, 19

MTV Video Music Awards (VMAs), 5, 24

NAACP Image Awards, 24
nominations, 5, 24

self-love, 16
singles, 21–22

"Truth Hurts," 5, 24

Answer Key: **1.** Answers will vary; **2.** Answers will vary; **3.** C; **4.** A

32